Go Seed, Grow!

Written and Illustrated
by Flora Carla Caputo

Dedicated to my late father,
who like the most tenacious and strongest of seeds,
bloomed where he was planted.

ISBN: 978-1-7365786-3-6
Independently Published
Created in Chicago, Illinois

It starts with a flower
singing to the bees,
colorful and bright.

Then magic happens,
at just the right time.
Petals curl in,
seeds peek out.
They need to go,
so they can grow
to make the world
green and alive.

A seed is brave,
when it goes.
It glides on the wind,
with a feathery wing.

It flies above the noise,
the gray cement,
the busy cars,
the close buildings,
searching, searching...

until it finds the perfect spot,
in cozy soil
bringing color and food,
to hungry bees and butterflies,
among the stone and streets.

A seed is clever,
when it goes.
it rains down
on the dirt below
easy and quick,
next to its sisters.

It sleeps under the snow and ice,
until it wakes in the spring,
and grows
making its family stronger.

A seed is sly,
when it goes.
It longs to explore,
taking a ride on a friend's pant leg
or a passing deer,
and enjoys the trip.

It hops off for a snug home,
to nestle in for the winter
and rise from the forest floor
in the spring,
all green and new.

A seed is trusting,
when it goes.
It knows waves and storms,
  or gliding fish, birds, or boats
won't stop it

from putting down roots,
to reach for the sky,

and soak in the sun,
to bloom again.

A seed is strong,
when it goes.

It bursts out like a rocket,
far out in the world,
to find a soft landing

then taking a breath,
　　from its exciting trip,
it beds down for a
　　　　winter sleep,
dreaming of
　　warmer days.

A seed is food
when it goes,
eaten by hungry birds
in the cold months.
They are thankful
to be on their way,
with their
tummies full.

Far they fly,
  leaving their droppings
      where the seeds
        find their way,

              back to the light,
                and the soil
              to start again.

A seed is life,
and life always finds a way,
through the rain, snow, and fire.
Against wind, storms,
smog, rocks, and steel
it breaks through.
it finds the sun.
it thrives. it blooms.
Wherever it goes, it grows.
Just like you!

The End

or a beginning?

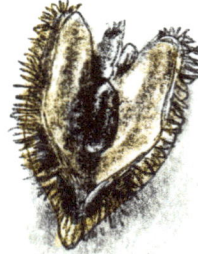

www.ingramcontent.com/pod-product-compliance
Lightning Source LLC
Chambersburg PA
CBHW061154030426
42336CB00003B/46

9 781736 578636